T0309500

APPROACHING THE
CENTER

New Issues Poetry & Prose

Editor	Herbert Scott
Associate Editor	David Dodd Lee
Advisory Editors	J.D. Dolan, Stuart Dybek, Nancy Eimers, Jaimy Gordon, Mark Halliday, Arnold Johnston, William Olsen, J. Allyn Rosser
Assistants to the Editor	Rebecca Beech, Marianne E. Swierenga
Assistant Editors	Erik Lesniewski, Carrie McGath, Lydia Melvin, Adela Najarro
Copy Editor	Dianna Allen
Editorial Assistants	Karyn Kerr, Derek Pollard, Bethany Salgat
Business Manager	Michele McLaughlin
Fiscal Officer	Marilyn Rowe

New Issues Poetry & Prose
The College of Arts and Sciences
Western Michigan University
Kalamazoo, Michigan 49008
An Inland Seas Poetry Book

 Inland Seas poetry books are supported by a grant from The Michigan Council for Arts and Cultural Affairs.

First Edition, 2001.

ISBN: 1-930974-01-9 (paperbound)

Library of Congress Cataloging-in-Publication Data:
Hardy, Myronn
Approaching the Center/Myronn Hardy
Library of Congress Catalog Card Number (00-134100)

Art Direction:	Tricia Hennessy
Design:	Jill Cianek
Production:	Paul Sizer
	The Design Center, Department of Art
	College of Fine Arts
	Western Michigan University
Printing:	Courier Corporation

APPROACHING THE CENTER

MYRONN HARDY

New Issues

WESTERN MICHIGAN UNIVERSITY

For Mom   Dad   and Erika
   this well   this beginning

Contents

IV

V

Acknowledgements

African American Review: "Comets, 1942," "Night of Chappotin," "Return to the Labyrinth," "September 21," "Inferno"

ArtWord Quarterly: "The Dirty River Between Us"

The Black Scholar: "*Nigger Out*: Rome, 1993"

Buckle &: "Swimming #1"

The Cafe Review: "Approaching the Center," "Familiar Distance"

Callaloo: "Africa Verde," "Granada Notebook #5," "Are You Langston Hughes?"

Curbside Review: "Dreaming in Antananarivo"

Many Mountains Moving: "100% Negro"

Quarto: "Conquest"

Third Coast: "Independence Day, Arkansas 1998," "Queen of Light," "Madagascar Notebook #2"

Visions–International: "Mosquito"

Wavelength: "Cachoeira"

The excerpt from "Map of the New World" is from *COLLECTED POEMS: 1948-1984* by Derek Walcott. Copyright© 1986 by Derek Walcott. Reprinted by permission of Farrar, Straus and Giroux, LLC.

At the end of this sentence, rain will begin.
At the rain's end, a sail.

Map of the New World
—*Derek Walcott*

I

Mosquito

She visits me when the lights are out,
when the sun is loving another
part of the world.

She passes through the net I sleep under   like
a cloud its holes are easily navigable.

Her buzzing tells me that
she doesn't want my legs   arms   cheeks
or chest.

No.

She craves adventure   wanting to travel through
the dark canal   the spiraling cave
where earthquakes are wind.

Her prize is in sight   the gelatinous mass controlling this machine.
How beautiful she thinks it is   her needle mouth
filling with water.

Her children will know physics   geometry   will understand
English   Spanish   perhaps Portuguese. They will be
haunted their whole lives by trees   guns
and a boom that won't cease.

She cries before drinking   the fluid is
salty-sweet. *Oh if my mother had
done this for me   I would have lived.*

September 21

my father pressed lemons   stirred their
juice in water   sugar a hail storm.
    Where are you going?
I took down the atlas.
    No. Where are you going?
    Home. To find home.
He looked away   I was an island
    Madagascar breaking from the continent.
The rooms dimmed   my mother watched the trees
fall   the sound cutting the earth in half.

Dreaming in Antananarivo

I'm following dark women
in pale head-wraps. They are
gathering bones   placing.
each in the baskets they carry
on their heads.

I'm barefoot   the sand
cooks my feet red.

They begin handing me skulls,
I'm dropping them   trembling with
ghosts passing through me.

Cinema

There is no more water left
in our glasses: only mint leaves
and stems   wet   mutilated   dark.

It is night. Men are gathering
in the streets. They are buying
caramels and cigarettes from blind
fathers   their palms gathering prayers.
The women are at home with their daughters
unraveling themselves   the secret
touch of air to body.

In the theater an American film never
shown in America makes the men cheer   curse Allah
when another head   arm   leg is lost to the gunman's
flawless aim.

We leave the theater and give our tickets to the
boys who stand outside longing for balconies   leather chairs
    the clicking of a projector and its sword of dusty light.

I'm listening to a song sung in Arabic.
The moon is a sickle thrashing through stalks of indigo.
There is only one star here: God's clear eye.

Five Pillars

1.

Green domes and doors
    the grass hill from where
we stare   a dusty city where
horns blare
    calls to one God.

I cut my hand on paper   a man with
his small son brings a finger of aloe vera
    its juice is cold yet I'm warm   amazed
in Gabriel's light.

2.

Before rolling out his carpet,
he finds east   his lost daughter.
He prays out of love   asking for
death   his body crumbling   flesh
filled with bees. He prays for his son
    a poet living in France who no longer
speaks Arabic. His mother cries when
he drinks wine   *he has too many*
women and doesn't want to marry any of them.

        Dad,
        Morocco is older than dead scrolls.

3.

The boy carries a scale. He places it on the ground
and asks people (foreigners) to weigh themselves
    two *dirhams* is the cost. I step on it   the dial
stops on fifty. I laugh handing the boy a ten
    both sides of his face violet as the closing sky.

I see Muhammad and Abraham   their clothes are dirty
    faded by the dry sun. They each carry a copper bowl.
The vendors fill them with couscous   fried potatoes
    peppers   chunks of lamb just before the
armless man gives them his shoes and dies.

4.

Allah fills their stomachs as they ache
    their heads spinning   prayers
    the Qur'ān in in their breath.

I'm quiet   they can't see me.
I'm thinning as they are   the spirit
holding us all.

5.

The   desert   dries   away   sins.

We   are   clean.

We have come with nothing but our palms.

Broken

The mirrors have shattered
           glass floats about the
room   life glistens in each piece.

You hold a heavy head
in your hands. No one
is dead   not
   even you.

Your daughter was the prettiest
girl in town. Her dresses   the
color of sky   her skin   the sun's
           fall.

Loneliness is war.

Don't worry.
                    Luck travels
warm in your veins.
           She will return soon
                    carrying constellations.

Cursive

I'm writing a letter to my father in the
Plaza Nueva   my sentences are heavy

with water   my woman has left me
I've had too much wine.

A gypsy drops rosemary on my
paper   India lost in her face.

She asks for money. My
tears darken my shoes.

I want to listen to the guitar. I want
to clap flamenco. Break this old

country's hex. My youth is too young
for Zorahayda's silver lute.

Granada, Spain 1997

1994

She got up early to hear birds.
It was her first time   their song made her close
her eyes   cool air   Homer's sky.

The graveyard Soweto had become was
alive   quiet though
the wisest man of all arriving east.

Passing Rhonda

He carries empty bags of seed   the burlap
sacks drag in the red earth. He eats figs
resting in the shade of the
yellowing palm.

In the olive trees   the swallows
    spirits
illuminate earth.

The white paint of the kitchen wall
curls off revealing the names
of the blue babies   the twins singed
in brass urns. His wife wanted to set
herself on fire after she gave birth:
*Ese cuerpo agotado! Ese cuerpo
maldicho!* she'd say.

He rubbed her back with oil   fed her
clear soup and fennel until she
could stand again.

On her birthday of that same year,
they made love until the honey came
back into her skin   her body
a colony of comb.

She planted lilac bushes around
the house   their scent brought
hummingbirds with pink bellies.
She grew her hair to the center
of her back   rows of tilled soil   the field
where they met.

II

Approaching the Center

It was after the islands of light
formed a continent   after Spain
became nothing more than dead
men feeding a vast olive grove
when we stopped to peel oranges   each section
a ship returning home.

Conquest

You buy vegetables on Calderería Nueva.
Sandalwood Os   mouths singing   sweet smoky
breath. I buy hazelnut pastries and remember

being stung while gathering honey in Florida   my legs
and arms spilling lava. I crush garlic   the scent
of the kitchen before the telephone rang. Your face covered

with blood   Jim Crow tightening around
your neck   nothing can save you. The zucchini and
eggplant lie on the cutting board in chunks   Moorish tiles

forever building Spain. I used to know
people in Mexico who wore feathers on their heads. They
thanked the sun when the maize grew and the
rivers ran thick with fish.

They are now drunk.

Their wives have black snakes for hair.
The men beat the women   girls   until their faces
crack   warm brown eggs.

Africa Verde

After your wedding
   mother made you a green dress.
Father gave you a gold necklace with
a whisper filled with peppers: *Never
take this off.* His dark hands on your shoulders   his
long journey to Portugal   mother held onto
his linen wrist for as long as she could.

You studied literature in Lisbon
and fell in love with a man's hair.
He fell in love with your dark skin   your doughy hips the
guavas he dreamed of when he tasted your breasts.

He kissed you before he left for America and gave you
his father's silver crucifix   the one his mother wouldn't
allow the undertaker to bury with him.

You waited for his return. You waited while your
belly filled with his moon. The apartment furnished
with books crawls with roaches.

You hock your necklace and take the night
train to Algeciras. Your feet have blisters.
You smell of musk. Mother's voice   hollow   old

Angola is so far away.

Call from Budapest

There is nothing here but
white paper   walls   loneliness
only the dead feel.

I don't know if there's light
outside or if gray rain is breaking
branches.

I haven't slept
this week and I'm so tired.

God
    if I could see the moon
just one more time
    maybe this life would change.

Junior, 1940-1964

When the asphalt turned to gravel
   the gravel into grass   the grass
into dirt   we stood in front of Robert's grave.

My father's ears burned   grandfather placed
his hands over the tomb feeling warmth
in all of that cold.

I walked away   unafraid of snakes
rattling their love. He was the first
doctor with our last name
   the thousandth who knew
young blood in an even younger country.

The first born son is either loved
the most or the least. My father   then a boy
   saw Robert's car stained with moonlight.
He cut himself on a shard of glass and cried
for his brother the way no one else did.

I will never know Robert
   a planet with a name yet lacking color
or landscape. Maybe he was the one I
should have known? The one who might
have made the world real for me   just once.

The Chicken Vendor

He saw them lay eggs and hatch
on Easter. He fed them white

corn   sometimes stale bread
when there was nothing left.

Today the chickens are fat
    white   the women who

dangle his gold continent from
their ears.

He puts them in cages   their feathers
blooming from glassless windows.

A woman bargains with him   *ten*
rands Ms.

        five

        six

he sells it for seven.

She sucks her teeth as it clucks in her bag:
    expensive, like this thing lays gold eggs.

Oh if it did (Nelson please forgive me),
I'd buy my country back   drive
these killers to the Cape as I change them to
stone. I'd listen with good hope for the sound
of their bodies breaking on the sea floor.

Granada Notebook #5

We sit down to black tea.
From the silver pot   the immigrant
waiter missing Algeria pours
the dark liquid into short glasses;
we soften its strength with sugar.
You tell us of your trip to Morocco   the veiled
woman who drew henna webs on your
hands   the short man who protected
you from his thespian friends before he stole
all of your money.

I imagine a rhinoceros graveyard   their hornless
bodies bursting with maggots for a white man's love   thick
knuckles   ivory rings on old women's fingers
writing poems with red and green thread   my great
grandmother sewing together swatches of her family's
clothes   passing its narrative on with a blessing:
fly away   fly away   fly away home.

The cool air brings Arabic children
singing with perfect Spanish accents.
During Ramadan they crave gazpacho and paella.

I will never forget the camel I rode
with my grandfather in Tangier   the stink
of its hair   its tall lumps shrinking as the sun
seethed   an Atlantic brimming with gold.

An Andalusian Tale, Three Parts

1. *Preparation: The Onset of Vision*

The old man wearing the ocher beret
carries a crate of brown eggs into
his store. The road is steep   made of field
stones and broken slate   a crocodile's back.

It is just after *siesta*. A German tour group takes
photographs of the cracked pastel buildings.
They stare at me. *I'm not part of the tour.*
The women upstairs are washing windows.

I'm watching eels swim up from the Darro.
Their black fins pop with blue electricity. They
are following a clown   his face is painted white
and red. He carries a gray cat on his shoulders   it cuts
his face before it drowns   suicide.

The Arabic men   their heads swallowed in
rings of white cloth are running with boxes
of apples and walnuts as a truck filled with
earth blows exhaust in my face.

2. *Incantation: The Arrival*

They called him the devil. The man made of shadows
and smoke. He rode into town on a spotted horse. They
said his eyes were unborn   heavy chestnuts. He played
the violin until the strings caught fire.   The women fainted.
He filled each one with an angry love   fading into their bodies
breath   light.

Their children had green eyes. The boys kissed their mothers
each night   wrote them love poems on holidays   grew purple
orchids in their yards.

At one in the morning
      yes   it was one in the morning when they painted
their faces with chalk and ash to slice their
mothers into six equal parts.

At one in the morning
      yes   it was one in the morning when they gathered
in the plaza to wash their hands in the fountain before
they flew home.

3. *Retribution: The Women Gather*

It has rained.
I see faces in ceramic jugs. I watch
women cry   their tears   rose petals.   Their
sons have left them.

I can see my mother's worry in the wood
frame of the street   the lines are thick   old.
I want to go home.

The clown stands still   frozen in his
gaudy gaze. His wrists are cut   lips of
severed women raped by an eyeless man.
His fingers have begun to burn. Crows fly
above him in a circle.

The mothers have gathered lemon branches.
They strip them of leaves and beat the clown until
he falls   he is torn   shredded   the knot in this blood river.

Familiar Distance

The Africans sit behind silk hills.
Spanish women tie the patterned earth
around their necks and bargain.
The men look at me. They are wondering
where I'm from   *how do I fit within their*
skull continent? I'm wearing my father's
leather jacket   the one missing the last
button   the one he wore throughout the 70s
    the decade I was born.

Their eyes are filled with sun. To them, I'm
American   a quarry of salt. I have always
seen myself as separate from my country's
red and white bands   its chiseled stars. I'm
part of a tar pit on the edge of toxic land   mute   dogwoods
sealed in glass domes.

I nod
    acknowledging their likeness to mine.
They notice the sea's changes in my
face   their great-grandfathers' odious
mistake   betrayal   a secret locked in an
ivory box.

I'm tearing up a map.
Its pieces fall into the Genil.
My hand matches the river's copper water.
I'm not home.

Madagascar Notebook #1

She sits in the doorway of the croissant shop
    her palm is curved as if holding a bird.
A father walking with his young son notices
her eyeless gaze. He places *francs* in her
basket silently sending a prayer to
his God   *death come quick*   *painless*   *let*
her fly.

Madagascar Notebook #2

After supper   just before the sun
closed its heavy lid   Alexandre played
his flute. The boys of the villages stopped
fighting and the girls folded their hands
in cotton laps. The elders saw their dead
bend from his silver pipe   their featureless
faces long at first then round with blind breath.

Madagascar Notebook #3

They stood in a pack
dressed in holy clothes.
Like wolves they fought over the *ramamamy*
the nun passed out just before
sunset   hunger controlled their fists
    their brotherhood lost in
hollow bodies on the verge of ash.

Nigger Out: Rome, 1993

The old city wall is chopped
into unrelated sections now;
even the pyramid stolen by
musty red men looks more familiar   close.

A dark-haired boy follows me into
the *gelatoria, Motown boogie
woogie, he says, Bella Italia.*
His teeth are marbleized.

Before school each morning
    his mother serves *caffe dolce* and
hard rolls for breakfast. *You are
American?* he asks, *Si.* I say

    ice cream melting on my hands.
I leave the store; its warmth like Aunt
Mott's cafe in Fountain Hill
    sweets forever. It is known that

Abyssinian women sell their bodies
to white men near the Colosseo   when
the moon is the giant light in black air.
Their husbands sell sunglasses and

pray not be cursed with another beige
child   adultery desperate and forgiven.
Across the street, lovers kiss under fig
trees. Their shadows rouse the

granite building smeared with the phrase:
nigger out. A friend, studying at
L'Universitá di Bologna   tells me of

one-hundred bald men marching

in streets: red sashes tied around
arms   combat boots   weights on
their feet. He tells his grandmother
of their uniform sound on stone

roads; she faints   Poland a gasp away.

Girl #1

When there was no more begging to do
and her beige soles were gray with soot,
she rested in her mother's lap to
have her hair braided. The girl
had waited all day to feel her mother's
fingers   affection in the tug of dirty skin
earth filling with light.

Letter Box

I place the letters I receive
in the box I bought in
Antananarivo   the wood
carved by the son of vanilla growers   his
fingers covered with dust.

The one from Beijing   I fold into
a crane   the postcards from Marrakech
and Jerusalem   I cover with a linen
handkerchief. My hand traces the
side:

>A woman pounding wheat
>in the village   her arms are
>thick   hard   a snake's body.
>Her children stand next to a rice
>paddy as her husband (their father) dies
>of malaria. He sees his mother's
>bones crushed by three-eyed
>babies   their dogs shitting in her tomb.

I write a letter to the boy:

>*How is your family?*
>*Did the crops grow?*
>*Is your art getting better?*
>*I'm afraid to ask but what more have you seen?*

My pen runs out of ink
as I sign my name. I
awaken dead glue
with my tongue   it is sealed.
I toss it into a blue mouth.

Tonight I hold the moon in my hands.

The Dirty River Between Us

I watch a woman sift through
kidney beans   pulling dark stones
from the piles of red in her hands. I
take a sip of water from the bottle   my
American stomach weakest of all. There
is a woman laughing with her friends. She
stands near the table of nail polish and
French perfume where the flies have
woven their knotty net. I point my camera
at her. She covers her eyes with a bronze
hand. *No. No. This soul is mine.*
She runs across the bridge; her friends
follow in a braid of smoke. There is a
dirty river between us   beer bottles   chicken
corpses   rotting fruit crates. She stares
at me from the other side. On her head
a wool hat where it's always summer   smooth
bare feet when they are always hard. She turns
away to buy little fish   their amber stares
premonitions of hot oil and onions. I
photograph the water before the bridge falls.
I look for her after I put my camera away
and know that there are only apparitions
in the day's last glow.

This Place

I ask for directions to the Camus center.
They wonder why I'm not
speaking Malagasy. *You look like us.* They say,
maybe you are from here. A long time
ago   from this place your people
arrived in America.

The Frenchman blowing smoke continents
into the air tells me that my president is
in South Africa   that he was in Senegal
earlier. *He walked through castles facing*
the sea shaking silver hands.
How hot it must have been.

I wander up a hill in a dust cloud.
I buy oysters from a dark-eyed girl
and eat them
with lime wedges.

I'm collecting stars
    stuffing them into my red chest.
    My marrow has turned blue.
What can I do with these white bones?

Comets, 1942

He watches women pass into the church
    their feet shedding daylight. They carry
bibles in loose fingers   the thin-skinned
pages exhumed from death.

He places his basket of avocados on the dirt ground.
A small girl stops in front of him   she'd seen him before
    in a grove of fog where Jesus waited
for the world to fall apart. She presses into an avocado
leaving fingerprints in its green ripeness.

There is a square in front of him where dormant
cannons aim toward the empty market   *tsy mitsahatra*
miteny ny maty.

He touches his tongue   the French he was
forced to learn in school after holding the bloody
hand of his headless father.

The church is white paper blowing to Jerusalem.
The earth is smoke gathering inside his palm.
He is shedding his skin in a pile   leaving it beside
the women who will never forget that year   those comets.

East: A South African Fable

They flew from islands   broken parts
of a continent   their wings splashed with blood.
Their eager chirping will turn to bullets
    break skin thick as clay.
The finches will travel at night
    day. They will find the sun near water.
They will take the trees   live within
the trees   the elephants will not
eat. Wherever they go a finch will sing:
    one   two   three   a heavy body will fall   fill
with worms   birds will pull   pluck until bones
are clean   chalk cracking.

I hear the horns of elephants.
Birds have taken the grass   ground   there
is nothing they can do. Their calves are domes
    mosques where east has crumbled

        no sky.

Their wings are plated with gold
but they are dying   bodies filled with
stones rattling.
    There is nothing here but war
      song splattering throats.

The Station

Peach light   finally.

They are waiting for a train
that stopped running years ago
    the track cluttered with
baobaos where lemurs play.

They are asleep.
They see fire and scorpions
    boats from

Indonesia

        Malaysia

            India.

The people here before

                dripping earth.

IV

The Man Who Fell in Love with a Bahian Woman

His Australia died in
her gaze. He'd found
a new country to live
        a new tongue to speak.
For her face was a
waning moon   shedding
light on the sea in his hands.

Soweto

1.

The women bring his body to
the market in bags   placing
him   cold   red   on wood
planks. There is smoke
everywhere devouring people
        we can't see anything.

2.

They have wrapped their hair in
scarves as they tend to the goats
        their pink dresses hiding torture.
There is a billboard of a woman
suckling her baby as the men beside
her prepare rice   chicken   slice
bananas and pineapples   barbed wire
above guarding empty apartments
as children's stomachs eat
themselves round.

The air causes cancer but nobody
has moved. Where would they go?
A father pours cups of milk for his
children   they die. He weeps until
weeds grow about his feet. He smokes
a pack of cigarettes and dies from
        anthrax poisoning

Crowd Control   is the

Truth

now there is

Reconciliation?

3.

There is a school made of tin   rocks
keep the roof from flight. *We are the*
children of Africa. We are the children
of Africa. They sing   as their teacher
claps keeping their steady tempo. Next
door there is a bar where men buy beer
     brandy and fuck whores in daylight:
look away children   look away   this
is not how you were brought into this world.

4.

There is a paved road in the center
of town. I'm following clouds   leaving
umber earth under my nails. I can't see anymore.

There are too many Christs here.

Return to the Labyrinth

We drink glasses of beer.
I notice the bartender's hair   thistles
ready to break   drift.

On the small television   we watch
the matador   his costume
seared in sunlight   thrust that mirror
    his sword   into the bull's back
already a sheet of red paper.

The tuna *tapas* we eat   wet balls of clay
quickly harden. The men at the counter
clap stuffing slices of ham in their
mouths   the cured meat
squeals down their throats.

We roam through the Albaicín in silence. The
orange trees bear green fruit. The heavy scent
of bitter olives
    relentless   my
grandfather's ghost.

We find a plaza   the Moorish walls
    ice white cooling away the day's heat.
        We sit
facing a fountain   its
spring   a dark mermaid gurgling.

The dogs stop barking   the old women draped
in floral cloth close their doors to bake bread.
The clothes hanging from the iron balconies
    tan chests wrinkling with

the release of wind. A half
moon illuminates the raven slashed sky. I mistake
Venus for the North Star.

That Christmas I got the telescope
    I knew every star
and planet like other boys knew baseball. On
my tenth birthday   my mother drew
Saturn on my forehead   space getting
closer and closer. That same year I fell in love
with the girl who smelled of apples

    her braids clipped with barrettes.
She took me to her father's farm and cried after
her favorite calf   Emanuel   was slaughtered. I brought

her cups of water   butterscotch
in gold wrappers   and rubbed
her back until my hands
wove their way into the cotton of her shirt.

If she were here   kisses
would travel from forehead to lips. I'd
hold her hand
walking to Sacromonte.

How she'd spin in her
chrysanthemum dress
    how this path

    air
            stone

would lead   on and on.

Cachoeira

Diego:
It was the sun that made me go.
I tore a ray of it into pieces and
ate each one. My eyes burned
saffron.

I woke up surround by natives   people
I did not know. They called me Caramuru.
I would live with them forever and marry
Catarina.

Our sons will have more of my
blood than hers. They will kill   grow
sugar and give this city a name.

Catarina:
I placed geraniums into
the sea before falling.

My dress turned
black   hair a school of eels.

There was no perfume in the air
*   only the brackishness of teal water.*

I drank remembering stones.

My people carried fire in wax hands.
They silently sucked in the
wind   their lips   numb.

Friendship

She finds her in the crocus garden
    face pressed in cow dung.
She looks at that dead creature   the woman
from cerulean and begins breaking
her wings   pulling each chestnut quill
from her back blotted with silver coins and blood.

She makes a hat out of them for her
husband's birthday. He places it on his head
then kisses her   sunlight passing through
dead skin. She makes him dinner   promises
nights in the Caribbean   the moon
becoming more and more distant.

When he falls asleep
    she unearths the garden   pushes her cold
friend into the hole then covers her with
all of that dirt.

In the morning there are zinnias and
cicadas tasting nectar.
    But all she sees is that ruined body
waiting to pull her under.

Inferno

Lazarus
    in Salvador your children sleep
on the steps of churches. They wait
for their sores to crawl off   leeches   ticks
too full for more.

No one gives them bread. The priests
and nuns pass every morning before
mass   black robes over false idols.

Tonight the police will gather their
lives   guns will spit   their steel
bodies blood hot.

They will visit you in Israel   they
will swim in the river Jordan. What was
that life? All of those palm trees   coconuts
    sky of violets I could hardly see   my hand
stretched out for another.

Genealogy: Lesson #1

The blond Jesuit spoke of
immigrants   his family
arriving on safe ground. We
were asked to tell where we came from:
a village   city   country   boundaries
cut with fingers.

My memory is lost. The mist above
the Atlantic is too dense the earth too thin,
but I do hear my grandmother's
secret voice. When we were under
pecan trees   the air sweet
breath:

> *My father painting stories*
> *with sand   his mother teaching French*
> *to her husband's people   their native*
> *tongues mutilated. Sending her*
> *son to Paris to become her father*
> *who held her dark hand after*
> *his journey from Dakar.*

For Hector Peterson

I have come to see the faces
    bullets turning to water   flowers
falling on children   sun   cool air.

I'm silent   photographs like fall
m e t a m o r p h o s i s:
    Soweto   Little Rock.

It's twenty-two years after someone
carried your broken body from that white war
yet soldiers still gather in this place
    guns burning in pallid palms.

Salvador, After 1888

Just past the Pelourinho   I stood
in front of all that blue
feeling blood underneath the street.

They wanted me there.
Perhaps they knew someone
I'd forgotten   the one who
gave me my eyes   the cleft in my chin.

Inside God was brown   his angels
too   sugar filling their mouths.
I removed the hat I was given in Morocco
and said a prayer   the first one since I'd
left St. Michael's. My friend told me that
his grandfather helped build that church.

I thought of my grandfather   the bricks he
pressed into cement the summer Arkansas
boiled over. The cross from
Bethlehem   its smoothness   God's hands
after life.

100% Negro

are the T-shirts the blue-eyed
brown people wear. The secrets
in the sugar cane fields sucked
into white roots. In the sun
we dance without shirts   only white
pants   throwing our legs in circles barely
missing necks   faces   arms. Those who watch
sing   pluck the *berimbau* and thump drums   rattle hollow
gourds. Not too long ago we sharpened
machetes on rocks   crimson lines keeping us alive.

How our art was banned. Those other
blue eyes so wary   fearful. It is the
forest   by ourselves where we re-remember
Angola   parrots flying above us.

The Gathering

Women in white dresses
fill the Pelourinho   Daniel's angels
in Rome.

One of their daughters holds
a blond doll by the arm.

From its cracked face
Iemanjá runs like blood.

Today is the beginning of time.

Beyond These Americas

I awaken to a window looking
through other windows   barbed wire
coiling over tops of fences.
The sun is my father acknowledging
me   making me grow. It is cold
here   crisp as leaves.

In Recife   I sit on the circus floor.
I watch a father hold his son   too close to the bars
        much too close   the lions take him   tear him apart
as father cries   women cover their eyes with
handkerchiefs. What beasts are these?

Have I become Herodotus? Cursed with his
saber eyes   bloody plume? I don't know if
he's the one I should be   if
I'm that strong. When that man was raped by

the police   I wanted to run away   erasure
set in my brain. In Georgia   in one or all
of the forests where men brought their
wives and children to see ropes break necks:
I wanted to run the other way. I didn't want to

hear their laughter   see the fire beneath their
skin. Even now the scent of pine makes me
gag   sometimes cry until all of me becomes
liquid   I sink beneath the earth.

In Texas   I roll with the wheels   men
are too dead to scream   too ill to understand
life   its bigness swallowed and passed.

I watch them   the dead   on their way
to the red island. Their bodies dry in the
sun   gourds underneath collect liquid. I run
in white sand as their mothers drink from those
gourds. The dead are wrapped in cloth   old
skulls guard their graves.

Women   their wives or their to-be wives
bathe in the Canal de Mozambique. Their
wet skin brings rain   pulls down clouds   the sky
is blue again. To the graves   they will wear

orchids in their hair. The wind will open its
wide mouth   they will hear secrets
that will keep them alive   feet just above
ground   feet always warm.

I watch them as I collect Aepyornis
eggshells   their line like the one to Oklahoma.

                    To the red island
                        to the red island
                        to the red island
they will go. Here they are.
Tombs open   they hold hands
    these women more than flesh   bone
will hold their martyred men
    hold them before they touch ground.

Here my woman is a butterfly where
the sky is purple. Here my woman waits
for me.

This island   this sea
    how red it is.

Joaquim, Prince of the Abandonados

I was left in a village. They say my mother died after she gave birth.
My father   drunk   quick feet   never existed. Rio is a wolf my blood
drips from her teeth. I'm always running   my feet raw   sole-less.
My country wants me dead   all twelve million of me.

If I could find a guaraná   I'd eat its berries and become a jaburú.
I'd live in the Amazon alone. The violent river would be my music.
    I'd stare
at Jupiter   call to him storm and all: *let me spin   let me spin*
in your eye   let me find Exú there and perch on his shoulder   worlds
    I could see
    worlds licked with fire   *worlds of perfection where I'd tear off my wings*
        to rest.

Swimming #1

We dive from mossy
rocks into the Gulf of Mexico   waves
dark hands cradle   cool
us from gold in air.

We see a sail and think of leaving
this island   drawing a continuous arrow
on azure. Oh what will we find?
Perhaps our mothers' country   their
faces in an anemone where clown
fish hide for safety.

There will be other islands   those made of ice   breaking
white as sun   land where snakes
cover rocks   their skins slick as tongues.
We will pass them as dolphins leaping from the
sea. On another we will watch ourselves play
clarinets   violins   trombones   our notes
     clouds that will rain. We will see
our unmet wives   we hold
their hands as our children follow.

With a school of angel fish   we swim in a bubble
of blown glass   they know us like these
currents   pushing all of us away.

Swimming #2

On coral three miles away
we found my sister's saint.
She was dressed in blue   lilies
floated about her long skirt.

   We thanked her for our
safe journey with bubbles from
our lungs   the lives within her
resting   rumbling in heavy dark lines.

Oh queen of secrets   tell us how those
boats felt crossing your body. Did they
make you scream? Did they numb you?
Did you want those captains to die   drown
   red silk to spin from their mouths? Please
tell me or if not reveal my dead family.

On a day when the sun is bright
let me see them in your waves   all
of them. How peaceful they must be   how soft
their gestures if any at all   their
faces calm as paper.

On that day   let me toss flowers over them   let
me cry if I must for this will be the last time
   the last time for me to know them   the last time
I will be willing to see the naked world   men
with fangs   blood in every eye. The last time
I will look back and cringe. The last time I will
hate in the dark. To history   I throw
olives and live.

v

To the Virgin of Regla

1855

He catches a yellow fish   her fins
cut his hand   he bleeds like Christ
    but no pain.

Her eyes are emeralds   he thinks
of jewelry   his wife's neck on fire
    the whole town envious.

He looks at the sea   its color makes
him weep. His tears make the water froth
    hands   arms   a face emerges.

She is made of wood   Augustine's fingers raw
with her   his Virgin forever in his mind even
after she left   453 AD burned into his skin.

He finds his friends. They help him pull her to shore.
They drench her in blessed oil. At night   seven slaves
watch her from under the great cebia. She is surrounded
by blue light   milk drips from her breasts. In the morning
they dress her in white clothes   they have made a gold
crown. They carry her on bare shoulders

                    mariposas blow in air.

2000

We take the ferry across the harbor
    we are to meet our new friends
at the church. We wait in the holy market.
There they are   dressed in white

entering the door   crossing themselves
with God. Saints hang on walls   babies with
their mothers kneel   pray. An old woman
tells of a boat that sank and birds that flew from the
sea floor   I touch the wall   the church in Arkansas
where my grandfather killed cancer   his
name carved in stone. The Virgin is behind glass   her crown
locked in a bank. She holds her child
      white Jesus in her brown arms.

We follow them through town   roads made of stone
      houses   buildings fading in sun.

            Iglesia de Nuestra Señora de Regla is
      the only thing in this small town. Do
      you speak Spanish?
            Do you speak English?
            We fished last night and caught many.
      We fried them in Habana Vieja and fed
      everyone on our street. My uncle played the guitar
            my cousin the drum   my grandfather
      claves.

We stop at the bakery where they work. The yellow
dough in barrels   flies breathing yeast.
They show us how to make loaves   our hands
rise and fall. I bake browner in this island oven.

A small door on a narrow road   we walk up a curled
stairway   the babalawo's house is bare   Africa
behind the door. He tells us of the people who see
him: the sick   the unloved   the haunted   the poor
      their stories blow into me   I'm cold.

There is someone screaming   someone drowning
    the water is so blue. He gives us beaded bracelets
    our wrists are heavy and we thank him.

Our friends lead us to the edge of town. We walk to the
ferry   a girl carries a decorated birthday cake on a sheet
of cardboard   I think of how her sister will smile   her
parents holding her hands   another year alive.

We buy peanuts in paper tubes. We eat them as we
speak of the saints beneath the saints   the earth
breaking its axis   all of this water   drink.

Interpreting Piano Lessons

From the yellow parking lot of Adler Elementary
and later St. Michael's   Thursdays my mother drove
me to that big mall in Dearborn   concerts glistening
on neurons. We'd take the glass elevator to the fifth floor
leaving popcorn breaking in air and scented
sprays prickling skin. In the Wurlitzer store
    I'd press the keys of organs   electric notes
    not rich or crisp like the piano in the living
room or the one in the store where Ms. Garibaldi
waited for me. I'd memorized the songs she'd assigned
    learned them the day before I came. The hour I practiced
everyday was spent on other songs   songs I composed or
heard on the radio unless my mother stood over me   *Für Elise*
    The Entertainer. You're going to be like your grandfather
she'd say.
    No. Not me. Rubén González didn't teach me how
to play. It will never be 1941   '42   '43 again (and that's
best for all of us). I will go to Havana but not Matanzas   at least
I don't think so. It would be nice to play at the Tropicana but
I'm going to be a writer. And even though this piano warms
your eyes   I don't like this instrument very much. Well   at least
I don't like it when I play. I hear how clumsy my fingers are
even if you don't. I can't be responsible for little girls   ballerinas
losing their balance as they dance around me. Maybe you will
learn someday   your father will sit on this stool with you
and play Tumbao   your new hand filled with rubies.

Academia De Ciencias Filosofia

I bought mangoes   took them inside
and listened to the philosopher
tell us: *Africa is our*
motherland Che all over his hands.

His young daughter sat beside him a Spanish
statue with Cuba's humid hue.
She made an airplane out of paper her
brother did too sharp creases ready
to slice *queso* air.

        Before we left it rained. The
boys outside didn't stop their baseball
game. The tennis ball still filled
the field with limes. They ran
the bases their shirts   newly
melted skin

.

From the bus window, I saw their
small hands push open the shutters as a palm
leaf waved from above
                one
                        two
like arrows from a loose bow
the airplanes flew. I listened
to them laugh and wondered how
long it would take for the
ripened coconuts to

                                  fall.

Father's Day

for Eric Hardy

He catches an octopus
and watches it die
   the sun burning its
purple skin   brown
   wrinkling.

There is no money for rum
or meat. When they ask me
   I have nothing to give them
but we are still friends.

I bought my father cigars   his
friends will light them up   smoke will lift
the room   *these are from my son in Cuba.*

        What is he doing there?
        Writing.
        Writing what?
        Poems.
        To whom?
        A girl who died when he was a boy   a girl
        whose hand he held until day ended: odes to her
        grave   odes to her long arms   odes to her
        favorite sea. He's probably writing those right
        now. Yes   in the Plaza de la Revolución
        his notebook and pen in hand. The
        sun is burning his neck. He laughs, My dear boy I
        finally know the man you are.

Poet in Havana

The tide rises.
I lie on the malecón awakened by lighthouse light.

The water is black   its palms
pull   release rock.

The moon is a grapefruit.
Brown hands peel its skin.

I eat the pink flesh inside   juice   love
                    fluid of souls
                                        God herself.

I can't believe I'm here.
Years   a lifetime of feet on loose ground   unfamiliar

air sanding me raw.
Why has it taken so long:

airplanes off course
                    trains   cars   buses unable to swim

equality too dark?

Four girls in school uniforms step over me   their arms
    rope-tied. They sing a rain song. Water splashes over us.

I'm awake.

It was ink and paper   locks on the doors
of rooms   the sun burning through my forehead
that brought me here. A boat made of poems rode

the sea   I so quiet in its cup. Stars dropped   cut
Spanish through and through; my skin
glowing under night's canopy.

I have written here   on this hard wall.
I have loved here   danced here   seen
water turn to wine   to blood here.

I'm awake.

When my boat loosened   I carried a stack of it
in my hand. I read the dry pages and thought
of a fire slowly doused   a low cloud licking wounds.
I was finally a writer   a poet in Havana.

No longer hated for my tattered road   no longer hating
myself   face scuffed with dirt and gravel.

I'm awake.

Their clapping is fluid in my head   drunk cells luminous.
Where am I from if not here?
Where do I live if not here?
Here where words are doves
                              here where poems are phantoms
drifting through air   sea.

The water breaks against the wall. I catch
a drop   it is the world.

                                   Here.

                                        Here I am

                                             awake.

                                                  Here.

The Visit

We rested at the malecón and
Roberto (thinking that we were Cuban)
asked us for a cigarette we didn't
have. He took us to his apartment.
His wife   a salsa teacher told us of
her friends in Martinique   how they
danced dripping balls of salt.

Roberto left to exchange our dollars for pesos.
Yerun told us of foreign men who come
to Havana for women   their lust for brown skin
older than any colony. They have asked
her as well   she thought of her child   the six
eggs lodged in the hill of rice on the
glass table and the poster of lobster   rum   grapes
on the kitchen wall. She ran home   her hunger
the oldest love lost in the reddest tissue.

She feeds her son spoonfuls of rice
and a fried egg. When he closes his
eyes she takes one for herself. His hands
are on her knees   his mouth a wide oval.
The steel plate is empty but he scrapes up
the few remaining grains   his belly round   a half
eaten melon.

Roberto returns. He offers us two
slices of *plátanos*   we accept   our fingers
hooks in his throat.

We exchange addresses before we leave. We will
see them on Thursday near the water. I tell them that I'm
a writer and they smile. I see

Yerun's beauty and hear the music Roberto must
have played for her   his drum dressing her in yellow clothes
conjuring her Ochún. In the dark, he fills her house
with azelas and his son wears leather shoes.

Quietly

Her legs are the roots of a
cebia tree sucking in old
water   purple memory
gushing through narrow veins.

A country of ghosts awakens.
They gather gems. They wait for
the bloodless by the sea.

Their hands are still.

Are You Langston Hughes?

she asks as I walk into the
Colina Hotel. *What?* The Havana
heat boiling her eyes   bringing back
a dead man perhaps the only
man she'd loved.

Does she notice the unfinished poems
fading on my cheek or did she see me
leaving the deck of El Moro?

Did she accompany José Antonio on his
fishing trip with Hemingway and discuss me?
What did they say?

Was she at my rumba party watching me
dance with pretty girls while she filled her mouth
with boiled bananas   shrimp   rice?

Did Nicolás Guillén show her
my translated poems in a local newspaper?

Doesn't she know that I don't look like
Langston? I'm from Michigan not
Missouri. I'm here to hold a
country in my hands then let it go.

Waiting

I tap the *bataá* near
the ocean   the waves licking the veranda floor
as the man in the guayabera shakes the *chequere*.

I'm waiting for them.
I'm waiting for women
to merge from the water   salt speckling
their hair. On their backs   they carry the babies they
couldn't years ago.

Their naveless stomachs
packed with rain.

Photograph of Angola – 1967

I was fifteen when I joined in
Cuba   a little bit older in Angola.
The palm trees were taller   greener.
I was stronger   leaner.
The guns we carried were heavier
and more women stood beside us.
In that Portuguese *casa* we spoke Spanish
and dreamed of *son* in Santiago.
How yellow we look.
How young we were.
        Africa older than forever.

Night of *Chappotin*

We ride into Habana Vieja.
The women brush off the dust
of limbless buildings. The men
are shirtless   selling mangoes
out of wheelbarrows.

A friend's love of the city plays
on the radio   the forbidden drum
of his country alive in this one   their hands
    warm   callused   shaken for the first time.

It is a plaza behind a church where we gather.
The grandson of a slave smokes a cigar   his
grandfather taught him sound behind the cane
               field
    the Gulf filling with phantoms   their
percussion echoing above water.

We drink rum with mint leaves
as they play. My eyes are closed   the familial sound
wraps me in red and white ribbons   with the moon
over me   tonight I dance   my feet caked with soil.

               Tonight I've found home.

Queen of Light

She eats green melons at a silver table.
From years of picking lemons
    the sun has drawn a spotted landscape
on her face   Andalucía.

With an ivory cane swung
above her head   she blesses
pigeons with flight   their wings
omens of luck.

The spiders have made her a webbed
crown. She is their queen. Her
back   a stone arch across
two worlds.

She is asking for *pesetas* in the
plaza. The foreigners shake
their heads as they drink
vino rosado and *cervesa.*

She has taken off her clothes   skin
hangs from bone   wet blankets.
She is splashing light in the
fountain   calling in a flock of birds.

They carry a vine in their dark beaks.
She wraps herself in its green body.
It splits   gypsy moths
on their way to the Sierra Nevada.

At Tom's Restaurant

for Natasha Tarpley

We have milkshakes.
People stare at my beret   the red star
making their eyes cock.

I see my first American sun.
The day clearer than the calls of roosters
in Guantánamo. We take a picture

in front of a Korean flower stand   iris
petals blowing about our almost-bare feet. You
notice my tan   I think of wind rubbing

palms   Cuba loosing her grip.

VI

Independence Day, Arkansas 1998

for Robert & Fannie Lee Hardy

I place a map of the world on the picnic table
    cornstalks spinning silk among the sunflowers.
History murmurs in wind. I trace the trail I took
    fingers crossing oceans   no waves
or sharks' teeth. My grandparents stare at the
ghost lands they've forgotten. Mississippi
    is their oldest memory   the house
on fire and the headless robins smeared into tar. My uncle's
barbecue flies above us and my aunt quietly hums a
    Stevie Wonder song.
My cousins gather fireworks   the sky cut with colored
smoke and light.

      This year   everywhere
looking but here   the swamp across the gravel road   the pine
trees where snakes climb   coil among the branches
    the rose garden where my legs were slashed when the horse
ran through it   me on the saddle unable to ride.

      This   place

      now
   roots of a willow   spreading all the way
    to Michigan.

Notes

Madagascar Notebook #3: *Ramamamy* is a Malagasy fried snack food made of rice and peanuts.

Return to the Labyrinths: Albaicín is one of the oldest settlements in Spain. It is a living quarter built over two thousand years ago by the Moors in Granada.

Sometime After 1888: Pelourinho means whipping post in Portuguese. This is the place where African slaves were publicly beaten and sold until 1835 when it became illegal in Brazil to do so.

100% Negro: Berimbau is a single-stringed bow musical instrument usually played as people practice capoeira.

The Gathering: Iemanjá is the saint of the sea in the Afro-Brazilian religion Candomblé.

Beyond These Americas: Aepyornis eggshells are found along the south coast of Madagascar. Aepyornises were giant flightless birds (now extinct) commonly known as elephant birds; they were about the size of modern day ostriches.

To the Virgin of Regla: A babalawo is the highest practitioner/priest in the Afro-Cuban religion of Santeria or Regla de Ocha.

Interpreting Piano Lessons: *Tumbao* refers to a composition by Cuban pianist Rubén González. *Tumbao* is also a specific Latin-Caribbean rhythm.

Night of Choppotin: *Choppotin* is a thirteen member Afro-Cuban musical group that specializes in the preservation of the *Son* musical tradition (an Afro-Cuban musical form). Many of these musicians are direct descendants of the African musicians who created *Son*.

photo by Lisa A. Cooper

Myronn Hardy, a native of Michigan, is a graduate of the University of Michigan and recently received his MFA from Columbia University. He spent 1998 in Soweto while researching apartheid and post-apartheid South Africa. His poems have appeared in *African American Review*, *Callaloo*, *Many Mountains Moving*, *Third Coast*, and elsewhere. He is currently working on a novel.

New Issues Poetry & Prose

Editor, Herbert Scott

James Armstrong, *Monument in a Summer Hat*
Michael Burkard, *Pennsylvania Collection Agency*
Anthony Butts, *Fifth Season*
Gladys Cardiff, *A Bare Unpainted Table*
Lisa Fishman, *The Deep Heart's Core Is a Suitcase*
Joseph Featherstone, *Brace's Cove*
Robert Grunst, *The Smallest Bird in North America*
Mark Halperin, *Time as Distance*
Myronn Hardy, *Approaching the Center*
Edward Haworth Hoeppner, *Rain Through High Windows*
Janet Kauffman, *Rot* (fiction)
Josie Kearns, *New Numbers*
Maurice Kilwein Guevara, *Autobiography of So-and-so: Poems in Prose*
Lance Larsen, *Erasable Walls*
David Dodd Lee, *Downsides of Fish Culture*
Deanne Lundin, *The Ginseng Hunter's Notebook*
Joy Manesiotis, *They Sing to Her Bones*
David Marlatt, *A Hog Slaughtering Woman*
Paula McLain, *Less of Her*
Malena Mörling, *Ocean Avenue*
Julie Moulds, *The Woman with a Cubed Head*
Marsha de la O, *Black Hope*
C. Mikal Oness, *Water Becomes Bone*
Elizabeth Powell, *The Republic of Self*
Margaret Rabb, *Granite Dives*
Rebecca Reynolds, *Daughter of the Hangnail*
Martha Rhodes, *Perfect Disappearance*
John Rybicki, *Traveling at High Speeds*
Mark Scott, *Tactile Values*
Diane Seuss-Brakeman, *It Blows You Hollow*
Marc Sheehan, *Greatest Hits*
Phillip Sterling, *Mutual Shores*
Angela Sorby, *Distance Learning*
Russell Thorburn, *Approximate Desire*
Robert VanderMolen, *Breath*
Martin Walls, *Small Human Detail in Care of National Trust*
Patricia Jabbeh Wesley, *Before the Palm Could Bloom: Poems of Africa*